The Song of a Satisfied Soul

'John Kitchen provides a powerful answer to the modern malady of discontentment. A larger house, a more expensive car, and a higher salary are simply efforts to garner bigger piles of perishable goods. John beautifully sketches for us the one true source of true contentment. It will make the reader see a familiar passage of scripture from a fresh outlook. A must for anyone searching for true satisfaction and renewal in a world full of need.'

Rajendra Pillai
Author of *Reaching the World in Our Own Backyard*

'There is always room on the shelf for another exposition of Psalm 23, especially when it is as balanced and practical as this one. The author allows the text to speak for itself as he reveals the richness of the believer's relationship to Jesus Christ. The ideal book for a pastor or other care-giver to share with those needing encouragement.'

Warren W. Wiersbe,
Author and conference speaker

'Could this be a local church's Book of the Month? Alternatively, could it be given at one of the landmarks of someone's life – on coming into church membership, facing a new challenge, or meeting with solemnity and loss? Here are fourteen inviting chapters, combining the learning of a Bible student's mind with the loving beat of a pastor's heart. Shot through with vivid illustrations and stories, "The Song of a Satisfied Soul" is going to end up at bedsides, in hip pockets, and handbags, and on preachers' desks. Let's wish it a long life in the service of the Good Shepherd.'

Richard Bewes
All Souls Church, Langham Place, London

The Song of a Satisfied Soul

Finding the Life You're Longing for
from Psalm 23

John A. Kitchen

CHRISTIAN FOCUS

Unless otherwise noted, Scripture quotations are taken
from the NEW AMERICAN STANDARD BIBLE®,
1960, 1962, 1963, 1968, 1971, 1972, 1973, 1975, 1977, 1995 by
The Lockman Foundation. Used by permission.

ISBN 1-85792-942-X

© Copyright John A Kitchen 2004

Published in 2004
by
Christian Focus Publications, Ltd
Geanies House, Fearn, Tain,
Ross-shire, IV20 1TW, Great Britain

www.christianfocus.com

Cover Design by Alister MacInnes

Printed and bound by
Rotanor, Skien, Norway

Contents

Dedication

To
Dean and Nora Kitchen

my father and mother

Your love, encouragement and support
have meant more than you will ever know

Preface

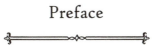

Sat'is fak's_hen: the state of fulfilled desires, needs and demands.

Got satisfaction? Get serious!

I am quite serious. Are you satisfied? With life? Marriage? Singleness? Income? How about your progress toward your goals and aspirations? How satisfied are you with the circumstances that have fallen your way?

As I asked myself these same questions, two polarized memories, long buried in the back recesses of my mind, unexpectedly collided into one another. The head-on collision in my cranium was startling to say the least!

The first memory to burst into my conscious thoughts was the mournful, discontent sounds of Mick Jagger and the

Rolling Stones. Brain-cells, not opened since my teen years, suddenly released the words and sounds of their rock-n-roll hit: "I can't get no satisfaction!" I can still see that empty, defiant look in Mick's eyes as he buried his face in the camera and announced to the world his deep dissatisfaction with all that life offered.

The second recollection to speed down the highway of my memory included the words of a hymn we sang at our church just last Sunday. Nearly one hundred years ago Clara Williams wrote:

All my life long I had panted
For a drink from some cool spring
That I hoped would quench the burning
Of the thirst I felt within.
Hallelujah! I have found Him
Whom my soul so long has craved!
Jesus satisfies my longings;
Through His blood I now am saved.

Mick and Clara were together in attempting to find satisfaction in life. Yet I am confident that Mick Jagger never sang any of Clara Williams' material. I am equally certain that Clara Williams could never have imagined any of the Rolling Stones' greatest hits. Though Clara and Mick were separated by the better part of a century and by an infinity of spiritual understanding, both speak for people today. Jagger has the most followers, Williams the more happy.

May I re-introduce to you another song of satisfaction? It is a well worn favorite. You may think you already know what it is all about. I am confident, however, that you will be surprised. Are you ready? It is the twenty-third psalm. That's right—Psalm 23.

The twenty-third psalm might well be titled *The Song of a Satisfied Soul*. It is a song I am confident Clara knew well. It is one that Mick probably heard, but cast aside. Perhaps that explains the spiritual distance between their lives. Maybe that articulates the reason for the chasm between their followers. What follows is offered in the hope that Clara's clan will sing her song all the more joyfully and that Mick's fans might change their tune.

I

The Shepherd of the Satisfied Soul

———◆◇◆———

"The LORD is my shepherd"
Psalm 23:1a

"The LORD is my shepherd" — even the most Biblically illiterate have heard the phrase. It's the line movie makers insert into the dialogue when they want to poke fun at what they consider to be the mindless and hollow hope of Christians. The phrase has become so familiar that many never pause to contemplate what it actually declares. Has familiarity, if it has not bred contempt, at least given birth to neglect? Could it be that our acquaintance with the opening words of this psalm has shut us off from their real power?

May we get basic? I'm wondering if we even know how to read the opening words to this best-loved psalm? Where should the emphasis fall as we pronounce the words? There are at least five different ways to read this line. Each reveals a different, subtle shade of the same marvelous truth. These five simple, yet powerful English words are represented in the Hebrew text by a mere two words. Yet their power has been proven in a multitude of cultures, over many years and in many lives.

Perhaps we should put the emphasis upon the first word: "*The* LORD is my shepherd." If we state it this way we are emphasizing the exclusiveness of the One who we are naming as our shepherd. We are stating that we have come under the care of the One and Only! We declare that the Ultimate and Almighty One is our guardian.

Not so fast! Can you say that honestly? Do you live in such a way that others can see you are confidently in the care of such a great and awesome Shepherd? Does your own heart know that kind of rest? It is true, we can say, "The LORD is my shepherd." We both know, however, that it is possible to intone the words without letting them get in touch with our hearts. We are more than capable of saying the words without truly believing He is capable of caring for us in the details of daily life.

Notice, it is also appropriate to put the emphasis upon the second word: "The LORD is my shepherd." Our English word "LORD" translates the most distinctive name of God in the Bible—the Hebrew name Yahweh (Jehovah in some Bibles). This is a name so rich in meaning that our English words fail us in trying to convey all its wealth. The name Yahweh reveals God as the self-existent One. Think of it! His right and ability to exist is not some external gift granted from outside himself. Rather He alone has the power of existence within His own Being!

The LORD is my shepherd

We depend upon Him for our existence, yet God depends upon nothing for His. Nothing can overcome Him. Nothing threatens Him. Nothing intimidates Him. Nothing can undo what He has decreed.

So wonderful was the meaning of this name that ancient Hebrew scribes would avoid pronouncing it or writing it at all cost. The name Yahweh represents so much of who God is that it was considered too holy for human lips to utter.

Yet this same God teaches us to say "The LORD is my shepherd"! Have you learned to live in the confidence of His keeping? Does the conviction of His care dominate your thoughts and emotions?

There is a third way we might pronounce these immortal lines: "The LORD *is* my shepherd." Emphasizing the words in this way stresses that God is present with me. It is to say, "In the midst of these circumstances, these events, these feelings, these problems, these challenges . . . right here, right now the Lord is still my shepherd!"

Enunciated in this way the line is a declaration, a confession and a reminder all at the same time. We are not saying, "I hope the Lord is my shepherd." Nor, "I think the Lord is my shepherd." Not even, "If the Lord is my shepherd I think I'll make it." Rather, saying it this way is an emphatic declaration: "The LORD *is* my shepherd!"

Did you notice there is a flip side to pronouncing the line this way? If you are daring enough to declare that this very moment you are trusting God as your shepherd, it necessitates that you are actively following and obeying Him. That is, after all, how sheep respond to a shepherd. If you say the sentence this way, it means you are vowing your trust and love to Him. Is that the truth? Honestly?

Consider the fourth possible way to state this timeless truth: "The LORD is *my* shepherd." Do you genuinely believe that He is *your* personal God and care-giver? Of all five potential ways to say this line, it strikes me, that we must at least say it this way. If we cannot say it with the emphasis on "my," then we cannot legitimately say it in any of the other ways.

Can you really affirm "The LORD is *my* shepherd"? Many read it, for all practical purposes, as if it says "The LORD is *the* shepherd" or "The LORD is *a* shepherd." Can you personalize it? Can you say, "He is *my* shepherd"? Does the pattern of your life show that He is? That you believe He is?

Finally, perhaps we ought to be reading Psalm 23:1 as "The LORD is my *shepherd*." A shepherd, in King David's day, was a watchman for his flock; overseeing the every move of his sheep. A shepherd served as a guard to protect the sheep. He was their guide, assuring full, satisfying provision for their needs. He was a physician who healed. He was a feeder of the flock. The shepherd, above all, was a lover of his sheep. There was an intimacy between the shepherd and his flock that modernized corporate ranching has robbed us of the ability to comprehend.

When pressed can you say with confidence "The LORD is my *shepherd*"? Ultimately the question is not whether you can say it this way—of course you can, God has made it possible. The truly important question is, "Do you?" The ability has been granted us by God through His Son Jesus. That actuality happens only as we place our trust in Him.

In the New Testament, Jesus is given three different shepherd-names. Jesus called Himself the Good Shepherd. He is also called the Great Shepherd. The Apostle Peter named Him the Chief Shepherd. Is He all of these for you at this moment?

Has a fresh look at this familiar line prompted a nagging doubt as to whether you truly know Him as you thought you did? Don't fear. The Shepherd is waiting for you to come to Him. Rest your trust in Jesus, the Good Shepherd, who has laid down His life on the cross for your sins and is alive and actively seeking to shepherd your life right now.

Which way should we pronounce it? Where should the emphasis in pronunciation fall? No doubt, were it possible, the emphasis should fall upon all five words—"*The Lord is my shepherd!*" While limitations of human language won't afford us that option, in our hearts we can affirm that the one and only awesome God of the universe is this very moment my personal and intimate care-giver.

Is your soul that satisfied in Him? If you're not certain, come with me as we continue to learn to sing *The Song of a Satisfied Soul*.

want anything. I do hear a lot of "If only's." "If only I had this . . ." or "If only I had that . . ."

Sincerely utter the last part of verse one and listen to the world snicker. "You have got to be kidding me," they scoff. With sing-song mockery they goad us, "All you have to do is trust Jesus and your every desire will be fulfilled!" Yea, right! They taunt us with, "You go ahead and stick your head in the sand. I'm going to go and make my own way."

It's unsettling, isn't it? We can rattle off this line of Scripture easily enough, but do we really believe it? Has satisfaction touched my emotions? Has it harnessed my desires? Can you honestly confess that satisfaction has seeped its way down deep into that part of you that no one else can see?

We are helped to discover that the Hebrew word which king David used here does not mean "desire." When we hear the word "want" we quickly equate it with something wished for. I'll admit that God has not given me everything I've ever wished for. Frankly, with the wisdom of hindsight, I'm thankful!

The word used here has the idea of "need" rather than desire or wish. This line might well be translated "I shall not be in want." David's point is that, if we allow ourselves to be shepherded by God, we will never lack God's perfect supply for our every need. That is a grand promise in these days of uncertainty!

But let's be honest—do we live in this place of contentment? Are we as satisfied in God as David seemed to be? What does it take to move from where we are to being totally satisfied in our relationship with God? I have found that tracing that little word "want" through the rest of the Old Testament helps open before me the pathway to satisfaction.

I shall not want.

The first step toward satisfaction is active obedience. David said in another place, "O fear the LORD, you His saints; for those who fear Him there is no want." (Psalm 34:9). Obedience is our part in allowing God to function as our Shepherd.

God never promised to meet the needs of the disobedient. In fact He says, "The righteous has enough to satisfy His appetite, But the stomach of the wicked is in want" (Proverbs 13:25).

God's provisions unfailingly fall within the circle of His will. When we choose, through independence or disobedience, to step out of the circle of His will, we find scarcity and want. If you remain within the circle of His will, the shower of His provision keeps right on filling to overflowing the emptiness of your needs.

If you want to take a shower you have to go to the bathroom and get under the showerhead. You can't take a shower plopped in your recliner. We need to position ourselves, through active obedience, where the provisions of God flow in a steady stream.

We move further down the path toward satisfaction when we realize that allowing God to shepherd us means opening up to other people. The Bible says, "If there is a poor man with you, one of your brothers . . . you shall not harden your heart, nor close your hand from your poor brother; but you shall freely open your hand to him, and shall generously lend him sufficient for his need in whatever he lacks" (Deuteronomy 15:7-8).

Built into the way God supplies the needs of His people is the fact that He often channels those provisions through other people. However, it is hard for some of us to receive from others. We don't mind God providing for our needs. We don't mind God using us to provide for someone else's needs. It's the humility required to receive His supply through the hands of another that is our biggest challenge. Yet part of being shepherded by God is being cared for by His people.

We draw even closer to a life of deep satisfaction when we discover that part of allowing God to shepherd us means allowing God to use us to shepherd others. The strange thing about satisfaction is that you can't gain it by hoarding. In the mystery of God's ways the more you gather to yourself the less you are satisfied with it. Benjamin Franklin once said, "The more a man has, the more he wants. Instead of filling a vacuum, it makes one. If it satisfies one want, it doubles and triples that want another way."

Are you willing to take some of what God has given to you and let Him redistribute it to others around you who are in need? It is not only God's means of meeting the need of another, but His means of loosening greed's grip on your heart. "There is one who scatters, and yet increases all the more, And there is one who withholds what is justly due, and yet it results only in want" (Proverbs 11:24). "He who gives to the poor will never want, But he who shuts his eyes will have many curses" (Proverbs 28:27).

Which are you holding closest—God or the things God gives? Willingness to be a cup, but not a conduit is the shortest path to dissatisfaction.

A life of true satisfaction also requires letting God be Himself. At first glance that seems to be a nonsensical

I shall not want.

statement—of course God is going to be God. God can't be anything other than what He is. He doesn't need my permission to be Himself.

That is not quite what I mean. You see our little word "want" from Psalm 23:1 is also found in the midst of a remarkable story about a man named Elijah. During an awful drought God directed Elijah to travel to a certain city and find a woman as destitute as he was. She had just enough flour and oil to bake one cake of bread. Her plan was to feed herself and her only son this last bite and then prepare to die of starvation.

When Elijah arrived God commanded him to tell her to make the last loaf of bread for him. Here's the shocking message he delivered to the woman: "For thus says the LORD God of Israel, 'The bowl of flour shall not be exhausted, nor shall the jar of oil be empty [that's our word!], until the day that the LORD sends rain on the face of the earth'" (I Kings 17:14).

Would you have believed God? Would you have delivered the message? Would you have accepted it? It went against all that was logical. Yet Elijah was willing to let God provide through one of His people, and the woman was willing to let God use her little to provide for another. Therefore she discovered that God is not boxed in to the way she thought He must provide for her needs. Most of us would have reasoned as she did at first, "I can't use the last for you! My son and I need it." Somehow she found the grace to believe God's promise, obey God's command and trust God for the extraordinary. When she did, what had been God's promise (v.14) became her personal experience and testimony (v.16).

God is creative in the way He provides for His people's needs. Don't box Him into the few finite ways your mind can imagine He must work. Active obedience to God and openness to others always yields satisfaction in what and how God provides.

There is one more step down the path toward total satisfaction—we need to cooperate with God. Repeatedly the Bible requires that God's people enter into the joy of labor. "'A little sleep, a little slumber, A little folding of the hands to rest'—Your poverty will come in like a vagabond And your need [there's our word again!] like an armed man" (Proverbs 6:10-11).

Satisfaction is not going to be found someday when your ship comes in. Satisfaction is not found in a winning lottery ticket. Idle plans about what you will do "someday" will never yield contentment. "In all labor there is profit, But mere talk leads only to poverty" (Proverbs 14:23).

I shall not want.

Want to be satisfied with life? Work! Being shepherded by God is not passive; it is active. You will discover that God often answers your prayers indirectly, through the channel of hard work and diligence. God still means what He said almost two millennia ago: "If anyone is not willing to work, then he is not to eat, either" (II Thess. 3:10).

Can you really move into a level of living where you "shall not want"? The answer of God is a resounding "Yes!" He desires to bring you to such a place of contented satisfaction. He stands ready to teach you to sing *The Song of a Satisfied Soul*.

the shadow of burnout,
I fear a breakdown;
But no one can see the real me;
Your expectations and Your people,
they goad me on.
You prepare a list of expectations before
me in the presence of my peers;
You provoke me on and on,
My cup seems more parched than ever.
Surely serenity and rest will elude me
all the days of my life.
And I will dwell in the land of the
harried forever.

Thankfully that is not the way David wrote it! Unfortunately that is the way far too many of us operate. Many believers are convinced that this is the kind of experience God is calling them into. A life of ceaseless, wearing, draining self-effort. A mind dominated by "I should's" and "I must's." A person who responds to life from such motivation is often outwardly indistinguishable from a person who has found the liberating rest of God. Inwardly, however, the spirit of these two lives are very different. One lives in bondage, the other in liberty. One operates out of fear, the other out of love. The one knows only weariness, the other rest.

David said of the Lord, "He makes me lie down in green pastures." He was free in the

Lord. He had reposed himself upon the divine promise of rest.

Notice that it is God who is making us to rest. That doesn't mean that He forces us to rest. Wouldn't that be an oxymoron anyway? Can rest be forced? Rather God is inviting us, leading us, inciting us,

He makes me lie down in green pastures

encouraging us to lie down and rest. Stop. Chew on that thought. Don't underestimate how completely backward that is from your image of God. God is inviting you to rest.

Are you heeding Him? Are you resting? Has it ever occurred to you that the thing the Lord wants you to *do* most is to rest? Are you at rest in Christ?

What words would your spouse or best friend use to describe what they see in your life? By rest, of course, I don't mean physical rest (though that is often included), but spiritual rest. God is inviting you to a spiritual respite that floods over into your emotional and physiological life.

Let's be honest, this kind of talk is a far cry from most of what we hear today about the Christian life. I must. I should. I ought to. But rest?

So much of what passes as Christianity today is rolled up in two words: "Try harder!"

The treadmill of twenty-first century Christianity can be gruelling. Guess what? God doesn't want you to try harder. He wants you to discover the rest of finding your all in Jesus Christ.

The Hebrew words here translated as "makes me lie down" have the idea of resting from exertion. It is the picture of reposing. Does that sound like the leadings of God in your life? If not, maybe you ought to rethink the source of those messages. Could it be your own ego? A misshapened picture of who you are? Maybe even some painful scar from your past that has wrapped itself around with misconstrued Scripture verses and told you that *you* have to work harder?

This same word is used elsewhere in the Old Testament to point to conditions that will be true in the earthly Messianic Kingdom of Jesus Christ. What a glorious future God has planned for His people! Rest. Peace. Fullness. Rest!

Amazingly David said that he had already entered into that rest, at least provisionally and personally. Deep

He makes me lie down in green pastures

within his heart David knew the liberty of resting in God his Shepherd. Do you? You don't have to wait for "someday." Listen! Can you hear His invitation even now?

Notice too that this is a rest "in green pastures." The word "green" describes grass that is young, new, fresh. It is the early grass of spring; tender, not yet burnt, hardened and weathered by the summer sun and days of drought. Can you see it? Have you caught its scent?

Imagine that soft, tender, emerald grass of an early spring meadow. Picture a sprawling valley of that young virgin sod. See it forming a downy bed of rest for you as you lay in the warmth of the summer sun.

When was the last time you laid down in the soft green grass, looked up into the sky and just rested, contemplating God, His creation, His goodness and your life? That is the metaphor David parades before our minds.

In Israel, as here, that tender green grass was a seasonal phenomenon. In spring the fields and even parts of the desert would come to life. In the summer and fall the sheep would spread far and wide to find food. Thankfully, God's rest in Christ is not seasonal, but His fields of rest are perpetual and constant.

David's verbal brush would also paint a picture for us of sheep, having grazed all morning in the spring meadows, laying contentedly in the grass in the heat of the day. No longer do they forage the hillside. They are at rest, regurgitating their food and ruminating contentedly upon it. There is time now to pause and gain the nourishment from what they have stored away in busier moments.

Chewing the cud is the best picture of what the Bible describes as meditation. Too often when we hear the word today we think of sitting cross-legged, hands turned upward on our knees, eyes rolled back in our heads and mindlessly chanting some mantra. That is not Biblical meditation. In true meditation we take in the Word of God through reading, study and memorization. Then in a quiet moment we regurgitate it (draw it back to our mind's conscious thought) and chew it over and over in our minds to gain all its life-giving resources.

All of this means, of course, that you must take in God's Word before you can bring it back up and "chew" it in quiet, restful moments of reflection. Listen to how David speaks of meditation elsewhere. "I meditate on You in the night watches." "I will meditate with my heart." "I will meditate on all Your work." "I will meditate on Your precepts." "I will meditate on Your wonders." "I will meditate on Your statutes." "My eyes anticipate the night watches, That I may meditate on Your word." "I meditate on all Your doings." "On the glorious splendor of Your majesty And on Your wonderful works, I will meditate" (Psalm 63:6; 77:6, 12; 119:15,

27, 48, 148; 143:5; 145:5). Sound like something you've experienced lately?

Do you see the point? God wants you to experience rest. "He makes me to lie down in green pastures." The problem is that some of you are noting down in your calendar or your electronic planner — "I have to rest! Make time to rest! Set aside two hours on Thursday evening to rest!" Then you will furiously throw yourself into an intense time of "resting!"

Do you see the problem? The rest God is leading you to is not a thing to be obtained, a discipline to be mastered, an elusive ingredient of the Christian life you need to discover. All of that makes for a contradiction in terms. The rest that God is leading you to is not a thing, but a Person. His rest is a relationship.

Perhaps the perspective of the New Testament will help. "So there remains a Sabbath rest for the people of God. For the one who has entered His rest has himself also

He makes me lie down in green pastures

rested from his works, as God did from His. Therefore let us be diligent to enter that rest ..." (Hebrews 4:9-11a).

Do you know this sweet, satisfying rest? Really? At the core of your being? Even in the midst of life's hectic pace?

Rest—it is the end of self-effort. It is the

end of trying to appease God. It is the end of trying harder. It is the end of the anxiety of measuring up. Enough of wondering if you are good enough! In the grace of God extended to you in Jesus Christ He offers you freedom from trying to be accepted by God. Christ's death removed all that hinders your acceptance before God. His resurrection provides proof of the Father's pleasure with Christ and those who rest their case with Him. Your faith ushers you into the transaction wherein Christ's own record of righteousness is credited to your account. You are free! Forever accepted in the Beloved!

Be at rest. He is. He has rested from His redemptive labors that you also might rest in His finished work.

4

The Direction of the
Satisfied Soul

※————◆◇◆————※

"He leads me beside quiet waters"
Psalm 23:2b

The sweltering heat baked their bodies and numbed their minds. This detachment of German soldiers had somehow become separated from the source of their supplies. It didn't take long for these battle-hardened men to feel the life-draining results of their prolonged exposure to the North African sun. With parched throats they stumbled upon a newly-constructed British waterline. Overjoyed by their good fortune they wasted no time shooting the conduit full of holes. As the water gushed out onto the desert floor they dropped to their bellies and began to lap up the water. By the time they discovered that the water that filled the pipe was salty it was too late. They hadn't reckoned on the fact that the British were testing the line with sea water. Inside twenty-four hours every German was literally dying of thirst. With no other recourse they surrendered themselves to the allied troops, defeated not by superior military strategy, but by nagging thirst.

In some areas of our lives substitutes will never do. Generic brands will suffice for some things, but there are certain cheap substitutes that inevitably leave us hollow and helpless. When loneliness, pain, fear, lust and aimlessness stamp their feet in demanding protest, it is easy to chase after the first substitute to offer us relief. In our haste we not only miss God's best, but we find ourselves in greater need than when we began.

Too often we seek peace rather than the "God of peace" (Philippians 4:7, 9). We settle for recreation rather than rest. We find a measure of happiness, but little joy. Too frequently we find a relationship, but not love.

I think of a sad verse from the Old Testament prophet Micah. Speaking of Jerusalem in his day, he said "Arise and go, For this is no place of rest Because of the uncleanness that brings on destruction, A painful destruction" (2:10). How sad. The very city that was to be God's place of rest—the city of God, the shelter to which people could come to worship the living Lord—had become a place of destruction rather than rest.

I wonder, could that be said of your Christian life? The very life in which you ought to find rest—the life to which others should be drawn because God is so dynamically alive—could it be that life has become a place of no rest at all? Could it be that God is saying, "Get up! Go! There is no rest for you here in this way you have been living!"?

I'm glad David talked to himself. It's a healthy exercise some-times. He ordered him-

He leads me beside quiet waters

self, "Return to your rest, O my soul, For the Lord has dealt bountifully with you" (Psalm 116:7). Occasionally we have to return to our rest. Could it be that rest lies not before us, but behind us? Sometimes we get caught up in the pace of the race and find that it takes more intentional energy to stop than it does to keep running. We need to re-establish God as our place of rest.

That was David's goal in penning the next words in *The Song of a Satisfied Soul*—"He leads me beside quiet waters." These few words describe the manner in which God is endeavoring to lead our lives. The single Hebrew word translated "leads" is packed with picturesque meaning.

When David said of God, "He leads me," he chose a word that underscored the gentleness of God's leading. The idea parallels that of being led by the hand (Isaiah 51:18). It is the warmth of God's extended hand that we are to see here. It is a word used especially of leading someone who is helpless or aimless.[1]

So often we picture God forcing us to do something we don't feel we are ready to undertake. It is true that God calls us to live beyond our human resources so that His power can be seen in us. Yet He knows your frame. He knows what you are made of. He understands better than you what you are capable of by His grace. Even though all-powerful, He leads with gentleness.

He leads me beside quiet waters

Is that not the essence of meekness—not weakness, but power under control? It is this kind of meekness that Jesus so wonderfully fleshed out for us. Though He is the very God of the universe, He had the infinite reserves of the omniscient Godhead under perfect control. Infinite power came under the control of divine love. Love became an expression of power and power served the purposes of love. That is how

God is attempting to lead you right now—with gentle strength.

A gentle guide is a wonderful companion, but most of us would also like to know where He is taking us. David's words also reveal where God is leading us. This same Hebrew word carries the idea of guiding sheep to a watering-place and inciting them to rest.[2]

Ancient shepherds did not normally "stumble" onto watering holes. They knew where they were located. These were trusted places that had proved faithful over many hot summers. These were locations known to be safe, secure and certain.

Is this not the way God leads us, His sheep, even now? No matter what the path God calls you to walk down, He is unfailingly leading you to Himself. Under our Father's direction we are guided to find our every need met, not in some cheap, quickie substitute full of loud promises, but in the trustworthy Savior Himself. All God's paths unfailingly lead back to Himself. Granted, obedience occasionally appears to take you into some desolate places, but it always dead-ends into God's heart. Your Shepherd knows that everything else you might attempt to fill your life with will simply not satisfy.

David's words reveal not only how and where our Shepherd leads us, but His motive in doing so. God's end goal for His flock is their refreshment. The words "quiet waters" literally mean "waters of rest." Translators have struggled to find just the right words to convey the meaning: "still waters," "quiet streams," "still and restful waters." The idea every one of them is after is that this place to which God leads us is to be a place of rest and refreshing.

God's motive in wooing you into obedience is quite simple, He wants you to rest. He wishes only your good. The only kind of water Jesus offers is the kind that satisfies. The fillers of the world may momentarily grant a measure of peace and rest, but soon they bite back and leave you worse than you began.

How perfectly Jesus, our Good Shepherd, fulfills this ministry of God! Prophetically looking forward to Jesus, Isaiah wrote, "His resting place will be glorious" (Isaiah 11:10). During His days upon earth, Jesus said, "Come to Me, all who are weary and heavy-laden, and I will give you rest" (Matthew 11:28). God promises that those who follow Him to the end will find that "They will hunger no longer, nor thirst anymore; nor will the sun beat down on them, nor any heat; for the Lamb in the center of the throne will be their shepherd, and will guide them to springs of the water of life; and God will wipe every tear from their eyes" (Revelation 7:16-17).

At this very moment, in precisely what you are facing right now, God will be what He has always been and what He promises He will never fail to be—your resting place. God is seeking you out to lead you back to Himself so that you can find all your needs satisfied in Him.

David honestly testified, "He leads me beside quite waters," yet at times he also had to exhort himself, "Return to your rest, O my soul." We are no different. God has proven Himself worthy of our trust. Yet perhaps this very moment you need to remind yourself of that fact. Do you need to put your hand in that of your Shepherd one more time? Will you follow where He leads?

Charles Spurgeon once related that in the deserts of the middle east, ancient camel caravans in need of water would send a lone rider ahead of the rest of the group toward the distant horizon. After that rider advanced a certain distance another rider was sent out to follow him. Then

He leads me beside quiet waters

another. So the caravan proceeded, single file, stretched out across the burning sands. When finally the first rider came upon water, he wet his throat just enough to clear it and shout "Come!" The next rider, hearing the invitation, echoed it to the third rider, "Come!" That rider then sent the booming summons to the next. Each rider took up the cry until the only sound to be heard along with the howling winds was a single cry: "Come!"

This is the cry of the Holy Spirit to your heart. Five verses from the end of the Bible, just a few words prior to sealing His inspired written Word to man, God announces: "The Spirit and the bride say, 'Come.' And let the one who hears say, 'Come.' And let the one who is thirsty come; let the one who wishes take the water of life without cost" (Revelation 22:17).

5

The Renewal of the Satisfied Soul

"He restores my soul"
Psalm 23:3a

It wasn't much to look at. Its paint was faded, chipped and completely gone in many places. Its body was covered with dings and dents, some parts were missing altogether. Rust was eating away at it like a cancer. It hadn't run in years. The ramshackle shed had been its isolated home for some time. As my dad and I looked it over, we both agreed that this 1951 Chevy pickup was a mess—but I wanted it! The seller assured us that "with just a little work" it could be a real dandy. Thus began my first lesson in restoration.

Inside of twelve months that truck was transformed. The embarrassment I felt the day it first rolled off a flatbed truck into our driveway had given way to the pride I felt as I drove it through town for the first time. Restoration is an amazing thing!

I think of that truck as I read David's next line: "He restores my soul." The words are simple enough, but we both know that restoration projects always involve more than we first imagined.

The word translated "restore" is a most meaningful one. It is used over one thousand times in the Old Testament and has a broad range of meanings—repent, turn, turn back, bring back, restore, refresh and repair. In contexts like ours it seems to point to the giving back of something that has been taken. It speaks of returning something to its original condition. It can describe giving back things that have been taken, like a man's wife, money or land. It is used of giving back a city or kingdom that had been captured. It described restoring a border that had been moved. It is even used of the healing of a body racked with sickness. It's the word selected when Israel is brought back to her homeland after being in exile. It's even used prophetically to describe the future reign of Jesus Christ on earth.

The goal is restoration to original condition. God, your Shepherd, is asking for your cooperation as He seeks to bring you back to what He designed you to be in the first place.

The focal point of this restoration project is your "soul." This too is a multi-faceted word describing, depending upon the context, the life, soul, mind or passion of a person. It comes from the Hebrew word for breath—that which is life itself, that which arises from the core of a person. Perhaps the most significant use of the word comes in the Bible's second chapter: "Then the Lord God formed man of dust from the ground, and breathed into his nostrils the breath of life; and man became a living being" (Genesis 2:7).

What does God want to restore? You. All of you! The trouble seems to be that we have our own *He restores my soul* notion of what the best condition for our restoration would be. My father and I had some significant discussions about things like paint color, wheels, and upholstery. I knew what was popular; my father knew what original equipment had been (after all he had been there!).

God is working to bring your thoughts into line with His original design for how the human mind is to reason. He wants to restore your emotions to their originally designed function and state. God desires to bring your will back to the design He intended at creation. God wants you to think with His thoughts, feel what He feels and choose what He wills. God wants you to be what He originally designed you to be.

What would I look like, if God had His way with me? Perhaps this very psalm helps us answer that best. What do we discover here that might tend to pull one away from what God originally designed for him?

This psalm speaks of insecurity. That insecurity is answered in God's promise to be our Shepherd. The psalm talks of our deep and profound needs. David, however, confesses that God so powerfully meets every legitimate need that we are never in want. Weariness is a concern. But food and water is God's answer. Aimlessness is a danger. God promises us His guidance. Lack of purpose is a threat to God's purpose for us, but God answers by guiding us to live "For His name's sake." Fear appears, but so does the presence of God.

He restores my soul

Throughout this song the singer of Israel describes God restoring him out of all the things that threaten to pull him from God's original design for his life.

Isn't that inviting? Shepherding for the

insecure. Supply for our want. Food and drink for weary souls. Guidance for our aimlessness. Purpose in our confusion. His own presence amid our fears. What promises!

How can I get from here to there? How can I cooperate with God in this restoration project? David said in another song: "The law of the LORD is perfect, restoring the soul" (Psalm 19:7a). Wash your soul in the water of God's written Word. David sang on: "The testimony of the LORD is sure, making wise the simple. The precepts of the LORD are right, rejoicing the heart; The commandment of the LORD is pure, enlightening the eyes. The fear of the LORD is clean, enduring forever; The judgements of the LORD are true; they are righteous altogether" (Psalm 19:7b-9). Sounds like restoration work, doesn't it?

There is a second related way in which we cooperate with God in His desire to restore us. In another song David wrote, "Create in me a clean heart, O God, And renew a steadfast spirit within me. Do not cast me away from Your presence, And do not take Your Holy Spirit from me. Restore to me the joy of Your salvation" (Psalm 51:10-12a). Restoration takes place in the presence of the original design, or perhaps better stated, the original Designer. You and I were made to share in the heart of God, indeed, in the very nature of God (II Peter 1:4). The most basic purpose of prayer is not convincing God of the wisdom of our ways, but aligning our hearts to His. Prayer is communing and communicating with God until our hearts are conformed to His.

We end up back at the basics don't we? Scripture and prayer—the key channels of God's restoration project in your life and mine.

I've always admired people who have the patience to restore antiques. It requires a certain eye. You must be able to see what once was and at the same time, what can again be. We need an eye for potential. No one is better at that than God. He's not looking for some hidden nugget of human potential still latent in your heart. Rather He still has His eyes on the original design and sees how He can bring you back to it. He still sees what He saw in the celebration of those first days of creation. He longs to begin the celebration again in your life. Want to join Him?

6

The Pathway of the
Satisfied Soul

*"He guides me in paths of righteousness
For His name's sake"*
Psalm 23:3b

The sign stood at the head of the trail. Behind it lay the vast western frontier. The warning sounded a bit foreboding: "Choose your rut well, you may be in it for the next fifty miles!"

That advice might hold not only for frontiersmen of the old west, but for one among us trying to navigate her way through the twenty-first century! Ever found yourself in a rut? Some ruts are unhealthy; not all of them, however. Rather than ruts you might know them as habits, routines, customs, patterns or grooves. Whatever we name them they remind us that we prefer form and structure over chaos. I believe it's a reflection of the pattern from which we have been cut. God and His ways tend away from confusion and toward order. As humans who function in His image, we too move toward patterns of behavior and thinking, ruts, if you will.

Caution is in order here, however! Our bent toward sin inevitably pulls the steering wheel toward the wrong ruts. The longer our wheels stay in them, the more difficult it is to jump out of them. I believe that is why David's words in the last part of Psalm 23:3 are so important: "He leads me in paths of righteousness for His name's sake." If we follow God faithfully, we will, to some degree, begin to find patterns developing in our lives. Paul called it "the law of the Spirit of life in Christ Jesus" (Romans 8:2). By "law" Paul did not mean a rule that, if broken, is visited with severe punishment. That is true of God's holy law, but that's not the idea here. Rather, by "law," Paul meant something that happens repeatedly. Take the law of gravity. The law demands that every time an object is unsupported in the air, it will travel in the direction of the ground. So is the "law of the Spirit of life." Every time we allow God to have His way with us we end up being blessed. Every time we keep our wheels on God's path we end up where He wants us to go. The goal is to get our wheels in God's tracks and keep them there. How do we do so? David's words help us understand the answer to that question.

It helps to notice what God promises to do before we worry too much about what we must do: "He guides me." The word translated "guides" is sometimes used to describe herding cattle to a predetermined destination.[1] The cattle drive is headed somewhere from the very beginning. Whatever it may feel like to you right now, God is not haphazardly leading you nowhere in

He guides me in paths of righteousness For His name's sake

particular, willy-nilly and for no special reason. There is order to His plan. There is intention in His counsel. God has a plan for you. What He does each step along the way fits with His overall plan, even when we don't see the connection to His conclusion.

The word "guides" also communicates tenderness in the guidance. While God has a plan He seeks to conform your life to, He does not lead with the raw power of omniscience, but also with the tenderness of divine goodness. God does not force us. He has a special touch—a shepherd's touch—that leads, but does not drive us. He is before you leading the way, rather than behind you cracking a whip!

In my early twenties I got my only true taste of backpacking in the Rocky Mountains. Our team was led through a beautiful mountain forest, past the tree line and up over 14,000 feet elevation. Only one among our group had ever been there before. He headed up our string of bodies as we made our way up the mountain. Every so often word would be relayed back down the trail of some dangerous footing or a slippery stone of which to beware. Because he led us, he always encountered any potential danger before we did. God too goes before you.

The verb in the Hebrew most literally speaks of God causing us to be led. The picture is not of the shepherd behind the sheep, prodding, goading, even beating the sheep. Our shepherd is before us, not behind us. How then can He cause us to be led? How can one cause another to follow them? Is that not far more difficult than pushing the sheep? Ultimately God causes us to be led by revealing the attractiveness of His own character. Our Shepherd is so compelling, one glimpse of Him and

He guides me in paths of righteousness For His name's sake

we want to follow! By revealing who and what He is, God creates a hunger within us, a hunger that can ultimately be satisfied only by knowing more of Himself. When He sets out, we, then, eagerly follow in His train.

That is all mental picture and metaphor. How, in practical terms, does that happen? Most often through God's written Word, the Bible. The same word used here in Psalm 23:3 is also found in Proverbs 6, this time in reference to the Word of God. After strong exhortations to build God's commands into our lives, we are then told "When you walk about, they will guide you" (Proverbs 6:22). "I shall run the way of Your commandments, For You will enlarge my heart . . . And I will walk at liberty, For I seek Your precepts . . . Your word is a lamp to my feet And a light to my path" (Psalm 119:32, 45, 105).

God's Word is that which both creates hunger for Him and satisfies that yearning. By feeding continually on it we can get our wheel in God's rut and stay in His path.

The word translated "the paths" actually describes a wagon's tracks. After time, when wagons repeatedly pass the same way, their wheels form deep ruts in the landscape leaving evidence of heavily traveled routes.

For that reason it's appropriate to call these ruts of righteousness. And by "righteousness" David probably did not have in mind so much the moral nature of these ways, though that is surely included. Rather he was insisting that God leads us in "the right way." The way He leads us through His Word will ultimately get us to where He will be able to bless us. These are "right" as opposed to "crooked" paths. Obedience never sends you on a goose-chase!

When I was a kid one of my favorite evening activities was to walk across the pastures with my father and check on our cattle. I recall well-worn paths on the hillsides, created by the repeated tramping of cattle's hooves. My Father told me that the cows knew the best path to take up a hill. If we would just follow their paths we would find the easiest way up and down the slopes. I doubted a stupid bovine had such intelligence. In my youthful vigor I would start straight up a hill, only to stop huffing and puffing half way up. My father, who had taken the well-traveled and proven path, would smile, remain silent and keep walking.

God will guide you in paths of maximum safety, though you may at times question His judgement. He guides you into ways that are equal to what He knows of your individual capability. Cross-country ski trails are identified according to their difficulty. There's nothing like getting on the wrong trail and having no choice but to finish! God never makes a mistake when we allow Him to lead us. Though we will sometimes wonder if He has overestimated our abilities, we will discover He never fails to provide all that is necessary for the climb.

Ruts of righteousness! Holy habits! That is David's confidence. Paths that always lead to the fulfilment of God's will.

He guides me in paths of righteousness For His name's sake

Why would God go to that length for you? "For His name's sake." To the Hebrew mind a person's name was synonymous with his or her character. We are, in one sense, God's reputation in the world. He has designed it to be this way. If you were Him, would you have entrusted your reputation to you? Make no mistake, however, thinking that God needs help in defending His name. Just follow faithfully. God is so faithful to lead you in the right paths and to tenderly shepherd you, that He is willing to let His reputation rise or fall based on how He guides you.

God is that good at what He does. He is that faithful. He is just that trustworthy. He has so committed Himself to you that He is willing to let His reputation ride on how He cares for you.

"Reputation," said Thomas Paine, "is what men and women think of us. Character is what God and the angels know of us."[2] God guarantees to lead you in conformity to His holy character. He does so, that, as people watch your life, His reputation on earth will conform to the reality of His character in heaven. God has determined to make you Exhibit A in His case to prove His trustworthiness to the world!

7

The Confidence of the Satisfied Soul

"Even though I walk through the valley of the shadow of death, I fear no evil"
Psalm 23:4a

As I stood at her bedside I realized that I was listening to the death-rattle. The morning began normally enough. The calm had been interrupted by a call: "Pastor, they say Grandma only has an hour or so left!" She was old. She had lived a full life. She loved and trusted God. But the "valley of the shadow" is still a frightening place.

Years before, I stood at another's side, this

time in the ICU. That day too had begun innocently enough; it too was interrupted by a phone call. As I made my way to the hospital I expected to find her in serious, but not critical condition, certainly not nearing "the valley of the shadow." What I found upon arrival unnerved me. There were no words exchanged, there could not be, given the tubes running from every available opening. But there was an exchanged look. She was a deep student of the Word of God, a faith-filled woman, and active evangelist. In her eyes that day, however, there was a horrified expression of wild terror. A look that seemed to say, "How did this happen? So quickly! Please do something!"

The "valley of the shadow" is a scary place, both for those passing through it personally and for those coming along as supporters. God, in response to the believing prayers of His people, restored

Even though I walk through the valley of the shadow of death, I fear no evil.

that woman to additional years of miraculous health. Years later, however, a 3:00 AM call pierced another quiet, calm moment: "Pastor, they say she has only hours left." God had once rescued her from that cold, dark valley. In the early hours of this morning He would walk with her through it to the other side.

It is true that for the believer death is not defeat, but victory. Yet death is still frightening. Death is an unknown to us. It is an unnatural thing. God never designed for us to face it. How does one face "the valley of the shadow of death"? How do you prepare for the times when the unknown presses upon you and casts its long, grey shadow over your life?

"Even though I walk through the valley of the shadow of death, I fear no evil." Those words have supplied the answer to those questions for countless believers in a multitude of circumstances over the past 3,000 years. Contemplate them a word at a time.

"Even though"—the words signal a concession. David was conceding how bad things could get. David was making his commitment to God with a view to the worst possible scenario. Have you?

Someone once said, "No matter how difficult you thought it would be, you always end up wishing it had been that simple." Life usually turns out differently than we plan it. Normal is normally nothing like we imagined. When you pledged your trust to Jesus, the Good Shepherd, was it in light of what you hoped would happen? Dreamed would come about? Planned your life would be like?

Be honest, life is nothing like you planned it to be. What has come of your restful trust?

Have you come to an "even though" kind of faith?

Jesus, "that great Shepherd of the sheep," made this same point to His disciples many years after David. He demands that our pledge to trust Him takes precedence over our family! "If anyone comes to Me, and does not hate his own father and mother and wife and children and brothers and sisters, yes, and even his own life, he cannot be My disciple" (Luke 14:26). Jesus insists that our trust in Him must come before our own lives! "Whoever does not carry his own cross and come after Me cannot be My disciple" (Luke 14:27). He requires that our vow of faith must take first place over our pursuit of things! "None of you can be My disciple who does not give up all his own possessions" (Luke 14:33).

No matter what, I will trust and follow the Shepherd! Is that the level of your trust? Nothing else will do in "the valley of the shadow."

Notice also the pronouns: "Even though *I* walk through the valley of the shadow of death, *I* fear no evil, for You are with *me*." This is no theoretical theological discussion. Because the possibilities are personal, so must be the pledge of trust. In "the valley of the shadow" a second-hand faith will not do. The faith of David's father wouldn't suffice. It had to be his faith. It must be personal!

When the doctor says "cancer" and you find yourself standing on the brink of "the valley of the shadow," the commitment had better be personal. When the pain, pressures and hardships are yours, the faith has to be too. Someone else's relationship with God doesn't offer much comfort then.

Till you take a long, hard look at "the valley of the shadow," until you can also feel its cold, damp dew upon your brow, you may be content with borrowed faith. But once you've been near enough to feel death's chill run up your spine, second-hand faith will never again satisfy.

Another key to peace in "the valley of the shadow" is found in the word "no"—"I will fear *no* evil."

Experts in the Hebrew language tell us that the expression used here means absolute prohibition. It is a factual, as opposed to only a potential, negation. What's that mean? It simply means that David's trust was *Even though I walk through the valley of the shadow of death, I fear no evil.* resolute, absolute, definite and firm. Absolutely nothing evil could conjure up would move him from his trust in the Lord.

How can a person make that sort of a definite decision? After all we don't know what the future holds. Isn't it naïve to presume nothing will ever come into one's life that is evil enough to make him fearful?

I suppose it would be possible to make such a statement flippantly, but I don't believe David was being presumptuous. He was fully conscious of the implications of what he was saying. We are not certain just when in the flow of his life's events David wrote this psalm, but it seems to ring with the tone of life experience. It would seem there is a track-record behind the assertions made here. David knew the score. He'd been around the block a time or two. He knew all too well the sort of stuff the enemy is likely to throw in the face of a child of God. With eyes wide open he demanded that it did not matter what Satan threw his way—he refused to fear any evil!

That kind of commitment is the kind that needs to be constantly fresh, being updated daily. The commitment I made to Christ in High School was sincere and complete. When I said "all" to Christ, I meant it. Through the years, however, I learned a great deal more about myself and what "all" means for me. I've also learned a good deal more about Satan's deceitful wickedness, the darkness of his kingdom and the unbounded depravity of his nature. So my commitment today, though no more sincere than the one I made in High School, is certainly more informed. When you say "all" to Christ, do so with the awareness that He will spend the rest of your earthly experience letting you in on just what the content of "all" is.

Ultimately, however, it is not what I know and understand about what "all" means. It is

Even though I walk through the valley of the shadow of death, I fear no evil.

what God knows it means. Only He knows my future. Only He knows what shall befall me. It was James Russell Lowell who wrote, "Behind the dim unknown standeth God within the shadow, keeping watch above his own." It was, after all, the Good Shepherd who said, "I will never leave you or forsake you." The "Even though" of our faith rests squarely upon the "even still" of God's presence.

8

The Companion of the Satisfied Soul

". . . for You are with me"
Psalm 23:4b

Study the following line carefully. What is it that your eyes decipher as you scan these twelve letters?

GODISNOWHERE

The rhetoric grew increasingly intense during a debate between an atheist and a Christian. At a climactic moment the atheist stood, strode to the blackboard behind the podium and in large letters wrote "God is nowhere." Thinking he had sounded the clarion call that settled the matter once and for all, he took his seat. The Christian rose, however, approached the blackboard and erased a single letter. He rubbed out the "w" and then moved it to the left, nestling it in close to the preceding "o". The statement now read: "God is now here."

In the line above, some of you saw "God is nowhere." Others of you saw "God is now here." The difference in the sentences is simply the misplacement of one letter, one space to the left. The difference, however, lies in more than the placement of one letter and a space, it lies in the perspective from which you view life. The difference in the way life turns out for us is infinite.

Vernon Grounds, commenting on the debate, clarified the sentence even further: "God is. Now. Here."[1]

The sole reason David cited for his ability to survive the "valley of the shadow of death" was the presence of God. Theologians have long debated the twin truths of God's immanence (nearness) and transcendence (exalted distance). Which is primary? Upon which truth should we focus? Both. His nearness is only significant because of His exalted and holy distance.

Another song writer after David asked "Whom have I in *heaven* but You? And besides You, I desire nothing on *earth*" (Psalm 73:25, emphasis added). The presence of God on earth is only significant because of His exalted glory in heaven. Indeed, that singer affirmed "As for me, the nearness of God is my good" (v.28a). The comfort in "the valley of the shadow" is that though He is near, He is also over that valley.

This is all the more clear when we view it from this side of the cross. Jesus, the Good Shepherd, has done more than come under the dark *... for You are* cloud of "the valley of the *with me.* shadow of death." He has succumbed to death itself! "The good shepherd lays down His life for the sheep" (John 10:11). Yet God "brought up from the dead the great Shepherd of the sheep through the blood of the eternal covenant, even Jesus our Lord" (Hebrews 13:20). It was He, who, after His resurrection from the dead, said, "I am with you always, even to the end of the age" (Matthew 28:20b). Jesus has passed through the valley, through death, back into life. He has been through and is now over that cloud of death. It is His presence alone in the valley that is sufficient to calm our fears and comfort our hearts.

What about when God does not *feel* near? What of those frightening moments when He *seems* distant, uninvolved, disinterested?

We need to remember that the presence of God is something to be cultivated. God is omnipresent. Yet we desire not only the knowledge of His presence, but also His manifest presence. A sage prophet once told a seeking king, "The Lord is with you when you are with Him" (II Chronicles 15:2). He went on to say, "If you seek Him, He will let you find Him."

Again, the truth glistens only more brightly under the resurrection sun—"Draw near to God and He will draw near to you" (James 4:8). Meister Eckhardt once said "God is like a person who clears his throat while hiding and so gives himself away." God wants you to know His intimate, daily, moment-by-moment presence!

The fact is that we are as near to God as we want to be. His presence is just as real to us as we want it to be. Any distance has not been created *...for You are with me.* from His side. Any reluctance comes not from Him, but from us. His invitation has been issued—"Let us draw near with a sincere heart in full assurance of faith, having our hearts sprinkled clean" (Hebrews 10:22).

J.B. Phillips wrote, "The presence of God is a fact of life. . . We may, by defying the purpose of God, insulate ourselves from that presence. We may, by unrepentant sin, cut off the sense of God because we are clouded by a sense of guilt. We may, through no fault of our own, be unable to sense the God who is all about us. But the fact remains that he is with us all the time."

The way has been made for us by Christ. The distance has been removed through His sacrifice of Himself. Now we may draw near in faith. Having drawn near, however, we must also cultivate His presence. His presence must become to us something we desire not just in "the valley of the shadow," but each moment and in every experience. When the singer said, "As for me the nearness of God is my good" he also immediately added "I have made the LORD my refuge" (Psalm 73:28).

In another song, David wrote "I have set the LORD continually before me." That is cultivating fellowship with God. For this reason He could go on to sing, "Because He is at my right hand, I will not be shaken" (Psalm 16:8). We prepare for those frightening moments in "the valley" by moments, hours, days, years spent in fellowship with Christ.

Short of the coming of Christ again, the day will arrive when both you and I will pass "through the valley of the shadow of death." Our experience then will be determined by how we have sought Christ and cultivated His presence in the present.

History has recorded the horrible deathbed-cries of those who have rejected or ignored Christ in this life. Altamont used his pen to turn multitudes away from Christ. On his deathbed he cried, "My principles have poisoned my friends; my extravagance has beggared my boy; my unkindness has murdered my wife! And is there another hell? O God, hell is a refuge if it hide me from Thy frown." The renowned atheist Voltaire cried out in his last moments, "I am abandoned by God and man!"

How different the experience of those who face "the valley of the shadow" with Him with whom they have walked through life! After a Christian astronomer died, his partner had this placed upon his headstone: "We have gazed too long at the stars together to be afraid of the night."

God is. Now. Here. Is He, for you?

9

The Comfort of the Satisfied Soul

"Your rod and Your staff, they comfort me"
Psalm 23:4c

Kathy was her name. A child. Homeless. Alone, except for the paint can that was her constant companion wherever she went. The people at the crisis shelter asked her about the can. "I'm sorry, this is mine. This belongs to me," she would simply say.

Urged to explain her attachment to the paint can, Kathy would say, "Um, not today." Whenever she was sad, angry or hurt, Kathy would disappear to a quiet spot, clutching the can, rocking back and forth. At times she whispered in low tones to the can when others seemed not to be watching.

Over breakfast a volunteer tried again to pry the mystery of the paint can from Kathy's heart—"That's a really nice can. What's in it?" "It's my mother," she said. "What do you mean, it's your mother?" "It's my mother's ashes," she said. "I went and got them from the funeral home."

Kathy went on to explain that she had never known her mother. Her mother had tossed her in a garbage dumpster when she was only two days old. She had been rescued and, through the long years of her short life, had floated between foster homes. One day she set out to find her mother. She was successful. "My mother was in the hospital. She had AIDS," explained Kathy. "I went to the hospital, and I got to meet her the day before she died. My mother told me she loved me," she said through tears, "She told me she loved me."[1]

Kathy clutched the only thing she had left after "the valley of the shadow of death." She was alone. That's what "the valley of the shadow" does to all who pass its way.

By now you've noticed the change, I suppose? David has passed from talking to others about God (vv.1-3) and is now talking to God Himself (vv.4-5). Why the change? Because the "valley of the shadow" strips you of everything and everyone! The valley leaves you naked, alone in God's presence.

God. Me. Loneliness? Yes, in regard to human relationships. No, in regard to the comfort of my own soul. God is here; here with me. Now. Is He enough?

God is enough; enough to comfort me in the solitariness of the valley. God is spirit. In the world of hard realities, what can He do?

David affirmed that in the aloneness of God's presence two things about Him bring the greatest comfort to the lonely soul. His "rod" and His "staff" are that source of comfort. Members of David's agrarian society knew instantly what he meant. Thirty centuries removed, we have to think a bit longer to see his point.

The shepherd's "rod" was generally a short, club-like shaft. Sometimes it was weighted at the end, covered with hardened tar, perhaps even laced with nails. The "rod" served the purpose of protecting the sheep.

Your rod and Your staff, they comfort me.

When a predator was on the prowl, the sight of the shepherd's club was a comfort to frightened sheep. Testifying from his experience with the sheep, David said, "When a lion or a bear came and took a lamb from the flock, I went out after him and attacked him, and rescued it from his mouth; and when he rose up against me, I seized him by his beard and struck him and killed him" (I Samuel 17:34-35). He had, "killed both the lion and the bear" (v.36).

He knew what a well-placed swing of the "rod" could accomplish. Though abandoned by all and stripped of everything, he found comfort in the protection of God's abiding presence.

The "staff" was also a comforting tool. The shepherd used the longer, thinner "staff" to guide the sheep. A poke or prod of the "staff" nudged a wayward stray back in the path of safety.

Loneliness can be disorientating. In the vacuum of aloneness swirling emotions can soon cause you to lose your equilibrium. With the loss of all familiar reference points, it is easy to wander from God's path. God assures us, through His "staff," "I will instruct you and teach you in the way which you should go; I will counsel you with My eye upon you" (Psalm 32:8).

Wounded animals are not easily guided. The pain of loneliness can leave one surly and reluctant to embrace the extended hand. Should we resist the guiding nudge of God's "staff," He may employ it for more extreme measures.

The same staff that guides may be used to discipline. The blindness that comes with wilfulness and disobedience, leaves us vulnerable to danger. A loving shepherd is willing to advance from a nudge to a prod to a spur to a strike, if required to protect the unwilling.

"All discipline for the moment seems not to be joyful" (Hebrews 12:11a). For this reason the "staff" may not immediately appear comforting to one chaffing under the friction of loneliness.

Your rod and Your staff, they comfort me.

". . . yet to those who have been trained by it . . . it yields the peaceful fruit of righteousness" (v.11b).

One more comfort embraces the soul when sight of the Shepherd's "staff" comes into view. The "staff" of a shepherd was also used to count His sheep. Periodically he would hold forth his "staff" and, as the sheep passed under the "staff", he would count them. The "staff" then became a symbol of the shepherd's knowledge of the sheep.

Just as the shepherd counted his sheep one by one, so too God knows you perfectly. When the disciples were panicked over the intimidation of their opponents, Jesus comforted them saying, "Are not five sparrows sold for two cents? Yet not one of them is forgotten before God. Indeed, the very hairs of your head are all numbered. Do not fear; you are more valuable than many sparrows" (Luke 12:6-7).

A German researcher once determined the average number of hairs on a person's head. The number varied, he found, according to the color of the person's hair. People with black hair had more hair, on average, than those who had red hair. More on a head of brown hair than black, and on blond than on brown. The average female head of black hair contained approximately 110,000 hairs, while a blond averaged 140,000.[2]

How long do you suppose it took the researcher to come to that discovery? Probably a significant portion of his life.

God knows you and everything about you in an instant. He does not learn. He does not gain knowledge. He cannot discover. He already knows. Everything. Instantly. Without effort.

Couple that perfect knowledge with His commitment to protect, guide and discipline you and you discover an amazing thing. Even in "the valley of the shadow" . . . even when abandoned by all . . . even there . . . even then . . . He still is there. That He is, is an inexpressible comfort.

The Calm of the Satisfied Soul

"You prepare a table before me in the presence of my enemies"
Psalm 23:5a

Has anyone ever wanted to take your job? How about your spouse? Anyone ever threatened your life with a weapon? Has anyone ever tried to inflict you with severe physical injury?

None of those scenarios is hypothetical to me. I can put a face and name to every one. They are called enemies.

We hesitate to use the word, don't we.

Enemies. It sounds so, well, unchristian. Somehow we've come to believe we shouldn't have any enemies. Jesus, however, never denied the reality of enemies. He sought only to change how we respond to them. "I say to you, 'Love your enemies'" (Matthew 5:44). Jesus identified them for what they are— "enemies." The Bible generally does not deny the reality of personal enemies. "When a man's ways are pleasing to the LORD, He makes even his enemies to be at peace with him" (Proverbs 16:7).

Jesus never promised that we would not have personal enemies. He only sought to regulate the way we respond to them.

Who are *your* enemies? If I allow my mind to linger very long upon those faces and names, bitter, ungodly, vengeful feelings well up quickly. Before I realize what is happening my pulse has quickened, my blood-pressure has skyrocketed, my emotions have turned vindictive and my mind has run amuck with ways I could have evened the score. I find it doesn't help to deny what people have done, but only to change how I respond to it.

How do I do that? Enemies harass. They hassle. Their goal is your destruction. How can you do anything other than worry? Defend? Hate?

The power lies in a promise. God will vindicate His own.

The verb "You prepare" begins to paint a new word-picture upon the canvas of our minds. No longer is this about the shepherd, now it is a picture of a host. The word is descriptive of the orderly arrangement of dinnerware at a fine banquet. Forks on the left. Knives and spoons on the right. Napkins neatly folded. Everything perfect. All is in its place. It's a word of order. It's also used of the meticulous work of the priests in building the fire on the altar of the temple and arranging the sacrifice upon it. It's used to describe soldiers in battle array. It's what a lawyer is after in the orderly arrangement of the evidence in a court of law.

You prepare a table before me in the presence of my enemies.

God takes as much care to order your life as any general in battle, any lawyer in court or any priest in worship.

Sounds great. Even better when you consider that it's done in front of your enemies. There is peace in that, isn't there? I mean, after all, if you are in the midst of battle you aren't going to be eating, at least not setting an orderly table. One eye will be upon the battle line. You'll be constantly checking your flank. You'll shovel the food in with one hand, holding your weapon in the other.

In the midst of even the most foreboding

threat, God is able to bring order to your life. If God can take a formless void of darkness and bring forth our ordered universe, then He can certainly order your life, no matter how chaotic it may seem.

Interesting, isn't it, that the same One who ordered the chaotic darkness is the very One who walked into the Jewish temple and observed a well-oiled racket that was ripping off God's people. What did the God of order do? He created chaos! Coins flew. Animals squealed. Potential sacrifices scattered. Tables flipped. People screamed. Heads ducked. All at the hands of the God of order.

When people oppose God, He brings chaos to their self-ordered rebellion. When we joyfully submit, He brings order out of the chaos others try to foist upon us. The knowledge of His sovereign order amid the chaos brings peace.

The image on the canvas begins to reveal that he has a victory celebration in mind. The enemies are now captives, defeated rivals

You prepare a table before me in the presence of my enemies.

who are reluctant guests at our victory party. The threat is over, the party has begun. Rest. Security. Relief. Not because we defeated the enemy, but because God kept His promise.

Bruce Larson tells of how he has helped

countless people over the years who have been crushed by the weight of making a life-changing decision. He would lead the anxiety laden individual from his New York office and down to the RCA Building on Fifth Avenue. In the entrance he would allow them to gaze upon the mammoth statue of Atlas. He watched their eyes study the model of perfect human strength. Every muscle is taut as the world's perfect man strains to hold up the world that rests upon his shoulders. Bruce would then say, "Now that's one way to live . . . trying to carry the world on your shoulders. But now come across the street with me."

Leading them to Saint Patrick's Cathedral he takes them inside to view a small statue of Jesus. He is pictured as a mere boy, perhaps eight or nine years of age. Almost effortlessly, the boy Jesus holds the entire world in the palm of His hand. A few moments of quiet reflection later, he would say, "We have a choice. We can carry the world on our shoulder, or we can say, 'I give up, Lord. Here's my life. I give you my world, my whole world.'"[1]

Does He hold your world . . . including your enemies and their threats? If He does not, at least don't be fooled into thinking that you do.

If He does, He will vindicate you. The words "in the presence of" picture our enemies sitting mortified in our peaceful ordered presence.[2] God will vindicate you. He will win. Therefore, all those on His side will come to victory in the end.

Don't try to dictate when or how God will bring the vindication. The Bible seems to spend more time showing David asking God to vindicate him than it does describing God actually bringing that vindication. Yet God unfailingly brings down the evil and raises up the humble and faith-filled.

Don't demand that God vindicate you. He's already promised to do so. Share your heart with Him. Be patient. Let God do it. "Never take your own revenge, beloved, but leave room for the wrath of God, for it is written, 'VENGEANCE IS MINE, I WILL REPAY,' says the Lord" (Romans 12:19).

Sooner or later God will vindicate you. He has more at stake in it than you. His very character, truthfulness and glory depend upon His keeping the promise.

Ours is but to let our souls be satisfied in the surety of His integrity. As George Herbert observed, "Living well is the best revenge." Let your soul be satisfied in this.

II

The Prosperity of the Satisfied Soul

"You have anointed my head with oil"
Psalm 23:5b

Poverty and prosperity are strange things. They're hard to define. I've glimpsed both around the world. A week ago I stood in a squatter's village that had been thrown up on an abandoned city dump in Mexico. Ramshackle shelters had been pieced together out of every conceivably useful scrap of discarded material. Garbage tumbled freely in the breeze across ground that was composed of some mixture of cast off trash and earth.

No sense picking up the yard. The earth consistently works new garbage upward toward the surface. The residents possess almost nothing.

I've visited bush villages in West Africa where the Sahara desert claims miles of new territory each year on its trek southward. The region is torturous. Ubiquitous red dust. Rainless days of blistering heat that can exceed 130 degrees. Swirling, vacuous winds. The powdery dust is the only natural resource. These people have nothing. Parents bury their children for want of a dollar's worth of medication. Is this poverty? If so, what is it I observed in Mexico?

I recall the rural village in Belarus I visited not long after the breakup of the Soviet Union. Seventy years of Communist rule had reduced the people to despair. Vast stretches of the landscape are still contaminated by the nuclear fallout of the Chernobyl disaster. What food they can grow further poisons their systems. Is this poverty? I tell myself it's one thing to be poor in a warm climate, another thing altogether to be so during a long Russian winter.

What of the small town in southern Argentina where my host exhausted a month's wages to treat me to a meal in his one room shack?

What is poverty? How about prosperity?

Where is the line of demarcation between the two? Or is there more than a line running between them? Perhaps a whole region separates them? What would that area be called? Contentment? Sufficiency? Satisfaction?

Could I offer a radical idea? Maybe instead of an area running between

You have anointed my head with oil.

poverty and prosperity, dividing them, there is one that runs through both, transforming each. Could it be that the label of poverty and prosperity, while not unimportant, is not ultimately all-important. Maybe there is a different kind of prosperity that is possible regardless of the lack of a physical address, worldly possessions, or a bank account. Perhaps there is a poverty that may persist even amid soaring stocks and compounding dividends.

David's next line, though it may not appear so at first glance, is a testimony about that kind of prosperity. "You have anointed my head with oil." What does that have to do with prosperity?

You may recall that when the Hebrews crowned a new king or installed a high priest, he was anointed with oil as part of the official confirmation of his office. Since David was king of Israel, when we read this line, our minds naturally race back to his anointing for that office. But we miss the point if we do.

How do I know that? Because the Hebrew word used here is only translated "anoint" this one time in the Bible. It means "to make prosperous," or, in their culture, literally "to make fat."

It was customary protocol in David's day for a host to welcome his honored guests by a ceremonial anointing of the head with perfumed oils. The act signaled one's welcome, acceptance and entrance into the wealth that the host possessed. It was intended to refresh the guest who may have traveled some distance under the hot sun and in dusty conditions. God is here pictured as the host, David is His guest. Note several significant facts about David's welcome at God's party.

You have anointed my head with oil.

The anointing is lavish. The verbal form used by David expresses an intensity of action. God is lavishly, exorbitantly and extravagantly welcoming us into His bounty. There are no parameters to God's wealth. Only faith limits the measure He will use to pour out His resources upon us as we do His will. What is more, God is eager to give. He is anxious to have you enter into His plenty. The hesitancy is on our side, not His.

A couple of days ago my youngest child, Clint, turned three years of age. That morning as I was alone with the Lord my mind kept racing ahead to the time when we would celebrate with Clint. For several weeks he would repeatedly tell me about his birthday coming and say "I'm going to get a . . . and a . . . and a . . . and a . . . and a . . .". I smiled in anticipation. I couldn't wait to give him the few things we had purchased for him.

I was anticipating the joy of giving to my son as I spent time with my heavenly Father. How timely that He had me reading Luke 11: "Now suppose one of you fathers is asked by his son for a fish; he will not give him a snake instead will he? Or if he is asked for an egg, he will not give him a scorpion, will he? If you then, being evil, know how to give good gifts to your children, how much more will your heavenly Father give the Holy Spirit to those who ask Him?" (vv.11-13).

My heavenly Father reminded me of how much He wants to give me. He did so by reminding me of how much I want to give my son! If a selfish, sinful guy like me has a heart to give to his kids, can you imagine how infinitely more desirous and ready God is to give to us?

We often assume God is less willing to give than we are to ask. Nothing could be farther from the truth! God is far more ready to give than we are to ask or ready to receive.

Notice, however, what He wants most to give—"the Holy Spirit." God is not interested in just giving us things, but primarily in giving us relationship with Himself. Things are not out of the question. But His meeting our needs through His own personal presence is top on the list of the good gifts He longs to give to us.

The promises of God have been given that "you may become partakers of the divine nature" (2 Peter 1:4). God withholds no good thing from those who seek Him above and beyond possessions and wealth.

Additionally, the tense of the verb selected by David is a first in this psalm. It may indicate that this bountiful anointing has already begun in David's life.

As mentioned earlier, we don't know exactly when David wrote this song. Was it written while on the run from Saul's murderous bands? Or was it penned while fleeing from his son during his attempted *coup d'etat*? Did it arise out of a moment of leisurely inspiration after his throne was established? Was it written out of poverty or prosperity? We aren't sure. Ultimately it doesn't matter. What we do know is that David has discovered a satisfaction in his relationship to God that neither poverty nor prosperity could touch.

No requisition orders. No demands. No more wish lists. There is a highway of contentment running smack through the middle of David's circumstances—and yours, if you'll care to look.

The party has begun. The oil of God's welcome is flowing. Physical prosperity or poverty can't touch this. The dance of God's goodness has begun this side of heaven, and the tune playing in the background is *The Song of a Satisfied Soul.*

12

The Saturation of the Satisfied Soul

"My cup overflows"
Psalm 23:5c

Here's a definition. Can you identify the word it describes? ". . . any of several physical or chemical conditions defined by the existence of an equilibrium between pairs of opposing forces or of an exact balance of the rates of opposing processes."[1]

Ok, maybe not. Try this less technical definition: "1. to soak thoroughly or completely. 2. to fill to excess. 3. To fill, treat, or charge with the maximum amount of another substance that can be absorbed or combined."[2]

Got it? Bet you do. Those words describe what we mean by saturation. It's what happens as the washing machine begins its agitation cycle—the clothing is completely immersed in water and cannot possibly hold any more than it does at that moment.

My cup overflows.

It's what happens with ice tea—at least if you are from the south. During my years in South Carolina I came to enjoy sweet tea. Sweet tea has so much sugar added that it won't all dissolve. The liquid is saturated with sugar. An icy mountain of white granules in the bottom of your glass—that's the way I like it!

So why all this talk of saturation? When David said, "My cup overflows," he used the Hebrew word for saturation. Essentially he was saying, "Lord, you've blessed me so much I couldn't possibly hold any more!"

Remember that silly, kind of annoying, old song that says the same thing? One line says, "If it keeps gettin' better and better, O Lord, I don't know what I'm gonna do!"

Saturation to the point of satisfaction—that's the testimony of the satisfied soul. Ever had it that good? A show of hands would likely reveal more people standing on the outside looking in on David's experience than those sharing it with him.

Is David describing what ought to be my daily experience? Or is it merely a goal toward which God is moving all things in my life?

The word for saturation is found only one other time in the Psalms. A look there helps us better understand what David describes here. Psalm 66:12 is a testimony of the collective experience of God's people: "You brought us out into a place of abundance [saturation]." Let's back up and take a run at it so we can note the context.

> You have tried us, O God;
> You have refined us as silver is refined.
> You brought us into the net;
> You laid an oppressive burden upon our loins.
> You made men ride over our heads;
> We went through fire and through water,
> Yet You brought us out into a place of abundance [saturation].
> (Psalm 66:10-12)

Can you make out the footprints of God in the sands of their human experience? The people of God did not always experience this overwhelming sense of blessedness. Count them up—six lines of trial, testing and hardship, only one of satisfaction. Their testimony, in fact, was that God often purposely led them into those difficult times. In the end, however, He always brought them into that place where they felt as though they were saturated with His goodness.

"My cup overflows"—did David always feel that way? Not at all. He had been ridiculed and rejected as the youngest son of Jesse. He had been hunted down by jealous king Saul who resented his anointing as the king who would replace him. David had tasted the bitter discipline of God after his sin with another man's wife. He knew the heartbreak of a child's rebellion and theft of his own kingdom. No, David didn't always feel like God had blessed him to saturation point. Nevertheless, God brought him to the point where he would confess, "I am saturated with God's goodness."

Science teaches us that in most cases a solvent's ability to absorb more of another substance increases as the heat is turned up. The saturation point goes up proportionally with the temperature.

This may sound a bit strange, but could it be that without the hard times we would be able to absorb significantly less of God's blessings? Could it be that the difficulties which God allows in our lives are the only way to raise our ability to enjoy and take in all God has for us? In other words, the hard times enlarge your cup.

Rather than concluding from the trials of life that God is less interested in blessing you, perhaps you should see them as tangible evidence that He will not settle with anything less than saturating your soul with all His best.

Your present circumstances are God's reminder that He is ceaselessly at work to bring you to this same point of satisfaction by saturation. There have been lean times. There will be again. All by divine appointment. God is at work through it all, directing your life's experience to the place where your ability to receive from Him is as great as it can be.

What is it, exactly, that I am to be absorbing? What is to be filling my cup? It would be tempting to read it as something concrete, tangible and monetary. It may include those things. The one thing, however, that God *My cup* wishes to fill your cup with *overflows.* more than anything else is Himself. That's right— Himself. Jesus extended the invitation to those in His day, "If anyone is thirsty, let him come to Me and drink. He who believes in Me, as the Scripture said, 'From his innermost being will flow rivers of living water.'" Ok, I know this is more metaphor, but Jesus went on to explain: "But this He spoke of the Spirit, whom those who believed in Him were to receive" (John 7:37-39).

Can God really make Himself so real in you that you just won't believe you can take any more? I think of what was said of D.L. Moody when he met God in a deeper way: "The power of God fell upon him . . . and he had to hurry off to the house of a friend and ask that he might have a room by himself, and in that room he stayed alone for hours; and the Holy Ghost came upon him filling his soul with such joy that at last he had to ask God to withhold His hand, lest he die on the spot from very joy."[3]

My cup overflows.

That was the turning point of Moody's Christian life. He was never the same. The people of God in every age, made thirsty for more of Him through His providential dealings with them, have found God just as ready to fill their void. He can do it for you. He will do it in you. He yearns to.

That which is saturated drips its excess. As precious as its solute might be, it simply cannot be contained any longer. God wishes to be that real to you. He desires to be that abundant in you. He longs to lavish Himself upon you.

There is a song that God longs to teach you to sing. It's not a trite, sappy little tune like, "If it keeps gettin' better and better, O Lord, I don't know what I'm gonna do." No, this is a song that emerges from dark days and lean times. The tones are rich with experience and fortitude. This is the sound of a soul saturated with the living presence of Christ to the point of satisfaction. Clara's fourth verse puts it this way:

> Well of water, ever springing,
> Bread of life, so rich and free.
> Untold wealth that never faileth,
> My Redeemer is to me.

> Hallelujah! I have found Him
> Whom my soul so long has craved!
> Jesus satisfies my longings;
> Through His blood I now am saved.

13

The Pursuit of the
Satisfied Soul

*"Surely goodness and loving-kindness will
follow me all the days of my life"*
Psalm 23:6a

Cotton ball clouds tumbled aimlessly across
azure skies as I peddled my bike along the
country road. It was a pristine summer
morning in my country home. I was making
my way to a designated, but nondescript spot
along an empty road where I would meet up
with some neighboring kids. Like every other
day we would hide our bikes in the tall grass
of the overgrown ditch and wait for the bus

that would take us country kids into town for swimming lessons.

The carefree serenity of the day was broken only by the anticipation of my favorite part of the trip. A long, steep hill suddenly descended and afforded the exhilaration of a speed unattainable by a grade-school kid in any other way.

As I reached the crest of the hill a strange sound pierced the veneer of my conscious thoughts. Deep, guttural sounds grew louder off to my left. Glancing about I spotted the source—an enraged bulldog charging my direction at full speed!

The gap between us was closing quickly. Just beginning to pick up speed as the hill dropped away below me, I added every ounce of effort my legs could manufacture. About halfway down the hill my speed maxed out. Casting a quick glance backward I saw my attacker: stubby legs whirling in a blur of impossible motion, gnashing teeth less than a foot from my back tire, streams of thick drool flowing from the flapping excess skin around his mouth. This guy meant business!

This day I would escape. Fortunately his short stride rendered him quickly out of the race. I found an alternate route home.

The memory remains vivid to this day. It has, however, become about more than simply mean dogs. It's become a metaphor about life's troubles. Ever noticed that not all bulldogs live at the top of a long hill? We aren't always afforded the advantage of built-in speed assistance. Some of life's problems attack us at the bottom of the hill. What then?

Got a problem dogging your heels? Marital? Parental? Occupational? Financial? Emotional? A quick glance backward just might reveal that they're gaining ground.

Ever had one of those dreams where someone is chasing you, but your feet feel like they are mired in wet concrete? The assailant is gaining

Surely goodness and loving-kindness will follow me all the days of my life.

ground, but you just can't get your legs to move! Then just as they are upon you . . . you awaken with a jolt!

Got a problem that just does not seem to go away? A difficulty that you just can't outrun?

David certainly knew what it was not to be able to shake a problem. Early on his greatest problem was a jealous king by the name of Saul. He had been rejected by God as ruler because of his sin. David had been anointed to take his place. The transfer of the throne had not yet taken place, however. Saul had no intention of letting it occur.

David served Saul well, but time and again Saul sought to take David's life. A casual stroll through the middle and late chapters of I Samuel uncovers David's frantic efforts to outrun the jealous monarch. Twice David dodged Saul's spear. He hid in caves. He feigned insanity in Goliath's home town just to stay out of reach of Saul! Twice David had the opportunity to slay Saul, yet he refused. He eventually lived with his Philistine enemies for a year and a half just to rest from the relentless pursuit of Saul.

David knew what it was to be dogged by a persistent problem. I share the details for two reasons. As a reminder that all those who walk with God do so with problems nipping at their heels. The other reason is that it sheds new light upon David's words here in Psalm 23:6. He wrote, "Surely goodness and loving-kindness will follow me all the days of my life."

The word translated "follow" means "to pursue". It is most often used of a man or group of men pursuing another with the intent of making war or taking revenge. It's a word for hunting down humans.

Throughout his life David knew what it was to look over his shoulder and see the relentless pursuit of persistent problems. Yet years of walking with God had trained his eyes to see something more in the rearview mirror. As relentless as were the problems, there were two other things which he had come to see as even more persistently in pursuit of his life. It was the "goodness" and "loving-kindness" of God. The word "goodness" is also translated as that which is prosperous, happy, pleasant, beautiful, delightful, glad, joyful and precious. The "loving-kindness" of God is His deep covenant commitment to uphold His promises of love toward His people.

In time and through experience God had trained David's eyes to see more than just problems and his emotions to experience more than simply panic. He had come to the place that, while not denying

Surely goodness and loving-kindness will follow me all the days of my life.

his challenges, he saw his privileges as looming much larger. Over his shoulder he saw God's rich goodness and deep commitment of love as persistently following him. Interestingly, the "Surely" that begins the sentence is in many cases translated as "only." God can bring you to the place where your persistent problems are overwhelmed and virtually obscured by the wonder of His perpetual promises.

Sound too good to be true? It's not. Ask Francis Thompson. His life began in privilege and plenty. His father wanted him to study at the prestigious Oxford University. Francis, however, had other things in mind. Before long his life was mired in an opium addiction he couldn't shake. He lived on sleazy streets and along the chilly, fog-shrouded banks of the River Thames.

Over his shoulder Francis discerned a legion of demons dogging him. Yet through it all Francis came to make out something more in the mists of those dark English nights. It's what he named *The Hound of Heaven*. David called it the "goodness and loving-kindness" of the Lord. Describing his frantic flight from God's pursuing Spirit, Francis wrote:

> Fear wist not to evade as Love wist to pursue.
> Still with unhurrying chase,
> And unperturbed pace,
> Deliberate speed, majestic instancy,
> Came on the following Feet,
> And a Voice above their beat —
> "Naught shelters thee, who wilt not shelter Me."

"Goodness and loving-kindness"—David embraced them as a believer. Francis fled them as a stranger, until one day *The Hound of Heaven* caught him. Through faith in Jesus Christ, Francis found something more lurking in those London mists, this time it was a

Friend and not a foe. You can find the same.

He's coming for you.

Do you hear the beating of His feet? Can you hear His breathing?

He wants you.

Don't run. He loves you.

Stop.

Turn.

He promises to reach you before the problems do.

The wonder of Divine love is that having pursued and captured you, He promises to pursue you still.

14

The Passion of the Satisfied Soul

"And I will dwell in the house
of the LORD forever"
Psalm 23:6b

Passion—not a popular word in many Christian circles over the last several generations. Passion was seen to be the root of a host of evils that would shipwreck any soul that dared attempt to navigate its stormy waters. Passion was the pulse of sin. Sin laid bare was fed by a pulsing artery running red with passion.

Oswald Chambers, however, had it right.

"The Bible indicates that we overcome the world not by passionlessness . . . but by passion, the passion of an intense and all-consuming love for God."[1]

And I will dwell in the house of the LORD forever.

Hear the reverberating echo as C.S. Lewis chimes in: ". . . if we consider the unblushing promise of reward and the staggering nature of the rewards promised in the Gospels, it would seem that our Lord finds our desires not too strong, but too weak. We are half-hearted creatures like an ignorant child who wants to go on making mud pies in a slum because he cannot imagine what is meant by the offer of a holiday at the sea. We are far too easily pleased."[2]

We do not ascend spiritually by denying our God-designed capacity to be passionate. Rather we soar when we direct that capacity rightly. The Christian life—the satisfied life—is not some kind of benumbed stupor. It is sensate, tingling with every spiritual nerve connected and carrying its full circuitry of feeling.

What is passion? It is that which releases energy reserves you didn't know you had. It creates vision where there was only myopia. It generates joy where there had been only a mundane sense of duty. Passion is the adrenaline rush of the soul. It is the stuff of which the satisfied life is made.

As David comes to the last line of *The Song of a Satisfied Soul* he arrives at that which is most basic of all—passion rightly directed and fully experienced.

Passion for what? For God. For the immediate experience of His manifest fellowship with us and in us. "And I will dwell in the house of the LORD forever" was David's final, triumphant shout. It is a declaration of hope, a testimony of witness and an affirmation of faith. 3,000 years later those who have moved into the satisfied life are still shouting about that same all-consuming passion. Nicolaus von Zinzendorf cried, "I have one passion only: It is he! It is he!"[3]

From the introductory strains, to the final resolving note, the passion to know and experience the fullness of God's presence is what *The Song of a Satisfied Soul* is all about. The first part of this sixth verse encouraged us to look behind and see the dogged pursuit of God in all His grace, love and mercy. This last part of the verse bids us lift our eyes and anticipate the experience of God's immediate fellowship in our remaining days upon earth and then His unrestricted and unhindered fellowship in eternity.

Think of it! This passion for His presence transforms every truth of our faith. Without a passion to know Him they are but dusty doctrines to which we tip our hats. Energized with the passion of divine fellowship they become the sweet fruit of the tree of life. Redemption is no longer simply about getting our sins forgiven, it is about residing in open relationship with God through Christ. Scripture becomes not a list of do's and don't's, but the voice of my Lord to me. Christ's second coming is no longer simply about escaping the frustrations of earth, but the joys of "face to face" fellowship with our Savior. Eternity is no longer simply about making sure your "fire insurance" is in order, it is about the wonder of finally singing in His fully manifest presence.

Eternal life is not simply a different life in a future, timeless realm. It's not merely something we will experience someday. Eternal life is His life as my life right now—"Christ, who is our life" (Colossians 3:4). "This is eternal life, that they may know You, the only true God, and Jesus Christ whom You have sent" (John 17:3).

Enjoying God's presence is our greatest need. The verb "will dwell" is from the same root word as "He restores" in verse three. More than anything else, David knew he needed to be restored to that place of personal fellowship with God. It is possible that he wrote this while separated from

And I will dwell in the house of the LORD forever.

Jerusalem and the tabernacle which was the focal point of God's manifest presence at that time. Whatever the actual events from which this originated, David saw being restored to the place of fellowship in God's presence as his most profound need.

Because of Christ, God's presence is no longer a matter of geographic location. He has made His people the temple of His dwelling (I Corinthians 3:16; 6:19). If sin has broken your fellowship with Christ, your greatest need is to confess it and enter again into the intimacy of obedience with Christ. If you have yet to trust Christ as your Savior, your greatest need is to be restored to fellowship with God through faith in Him.

Enjoying God's presence is our greatest privilege. David did not take fellowship with God for granted. He anticipated an everlasting future spent in the presence of God.

If you could do anything forever—and only that one thing—what would it be? For David it would be open, unhindered relationship with God. David also wrote, "One thing I have asked from the LORD, that I shall seek: That I may dwell in the house of the LORD all the days of my life, To behold the beauty of the LORD And to meditate in His temple" (Psalm 27:4). Elsewhere he sang, "How blessed is the one whom You choose and bring near to You To dwell in Your courts. We will be satisfied with the goodness of Your house, Your holy temple" (Psalm 65:4).

Enjoying God's presence is our greatest security. As David brings to a close this song of assurance and safety his final notes emphasize the security of life lived in God's presence.

We heard of David's longing for God's presence in Psalm 27:4. The two verses that follow make clear just why he so yearned for Him: "For in the day of trouble He will conceal me in His tabernacle; In the secret place of His tent He will hide me; He will lift me up on a rock. And now my head will be lifted up above my enemies around me, And I will offer in His tent sacrifices with shouts of joy; I will sing, yes, I will sing praises to the LORD" (Psalm 27:5-6).

The presence of God—abiding with Him in open, unhindered fellowship in the center of His will—is the safest place on earth.

Enjoying God's presence is our greatest hope. David's anticipation was that He would enjoy this divine fellowship "forever." Literally the words are "for length of days." As David contemplated however many days he might have remaining and whatever those remaining days might hold, he confidently believed that not one of those days would pass but that he would know the immediate, personal presence of His God. The span of this hope, however, reaches far beyond time and space. Our hope extends into the limitless days of eternity: "For this reason, they are before the throne of God; and they serve Him day and night in His temple; and He who sits on the throne will spread His tabernacle over them. They will hunger no longer, nor thirst any-

And I will dwell in the house of the Lord forever.

more; nor will the sun beat down on them, nor any heat; for the Lamb in the center of the throne will be their shepherd, and will guide them to the springs of the water of life; and God will wipe every tear from their eyes" (Revelation 7:15-17).

When we begin to enter into the satisfied life we discover that we are living not in the beginning of the end, nor even at the end of the beginning, but at the beginning of everything!

He is our passion. *He* is our greatest need, our most profound privilege, our surest security, and our highest hope. The satisfied life is not found in the absence of all want, but in the focus of our want upon the only One who can satisfy. The truly satisfied life is not about wanting nothing, but about wanting Him . . . and perpetually finding Him. It is about being delightfully satisfied in Him every time we do. He satisfies. Only

He satisfies. He satisfies not by obliterating all want, but by deepening our want for Himself.

He is the satisfied life. He is the subject of our soul's song. He, living within us, is *The Song of the Satisfied Soul*.

Hallelujah! I have found Him
Whom my soul so long has craved!
Jesus satisfies my longings;
Through His blood I now am saved.

Psalm 23

A *Psalm of David.*

1

The LORD is my shepherd,
I shall not want.

2

He makes me lie down in green pastures;
He leads me beside quiet waters.

3

He restores my soul;
He guides me in the paths of righteousness
For His name's sake.

4

Even though I walk through the
valley of the shadow of death,
I fear no evil, for You are with me;
Your rod and Your staff, they comfort me.

5

You prepare a table before me in the
presence of my enemies;
You have anointed my head with oil;
My cup overflows.

6

Surely goodness and loving-kindness will
follow me all the days of my life,
And I will dwell in the
house of the LORD forever.

ENDNOTES

Chapter 4

1. Coppes, Leonard J., "נָהַל‎," *Theological Wordbook of the Old Testament* (Chicago: Moody Press, 1980), 2:559.
2. Ibid.

Chapter 6

1. Coppes, Leonard J., "נָחָה‎," *Theological Wordbook of the Old Testament* (Chicago: Moody Press, 1980), 2:568-569.
2. Draper, Edythe, *Draper's Book of Quotations for the Christian World* (Wheaton, Illinois: Tyndale House Publishers, Inc., 1992), 530.

Chapter 8

1. Quoted in "Reflections," *Christianity Today*, January 8, 1996, p.53.

Chapter 9

1. Letter from Covenant House, 346 West 17th Street, New York, New York, 10011-5002.
2. Tan, Paul Lee, *Encyclopedia of 7,700 Illustrations: Signs of the Times* (Rockville, Maryland: Assurance Publishers, 1979), 494.

Chapter 10

1. Larson, Bruce, *Believe and Belong* (Grand Rapids, Michigan: Fleming H. Revell Company, 1982).
2. Brown, Francis, S.R. Driver, Charles A. Briggs, *A Hebrew and English Lexicon of the Old Testament* (Oxford: Clarendon Press, n.d.), 617.

Chapter 12

1. "Saturation," *The New Encyclopaedia Britannica*, 1998.

2. Stein, Jess, editor in chief, *The Random House Dictionary* (New York: Ballantine Books, 1980), 794.

3. Taken from *Ablaze For God* by Wesley L. Duewel © 1989 by *Wesley L. Duewel*. Used by permission of Zondervan.

Chapter 14

1. Verploegh, Harry, ed., *Oswald Chambers: The Best From All His Books* (Nashville: Oliver Nelson, 1987), 233.

2. Lewis, C.S., *The Quotable Lewis* (Wheaton, Illinois: Tyndale House Publishers, Inc., 1989), 352.

3. Draper, Edythe, *Draper's Book of Quotations for the Christian World* (Wheaton, Illinois: Tyndale House Publishers, Inc., 1992), 349.

About the Author

John Kitchen grew up on the plains of rural Iowa. After coming to faith in Christ, John sensed God's call on his life. John is the Senior Pastor of the Stow Alliance Fellowship in Stow, Ohio. John holds degrees from Crown College (B.A.), Columbia Biblical Seminary (M.Div.) and Trinity Evangelical Divinity School (D.Min.). He is joyfully married to Julie and together they enjoy their children Melody, Joe and Clint. Time with family, reading, the outdoors and cycling are among his favorite things in life.

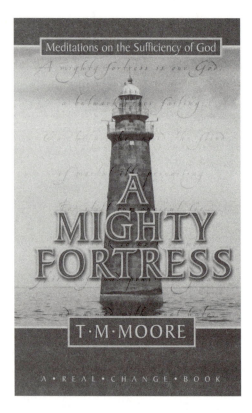

Meditations on the Sufficiency of God

A
MIGHTY
FORTRESS

T·M·MOORE

A · REAL · CHANGE · BOOK

A Mighty Fortress

Meditations on the Sufficiency of God

T. M. Moore

A Real Change book

God writes a lyric through our life. Through the means of praise and worship we can express our spiritual yearnings in ways that we would find difficult in everyday words or conversation.

Yet lyrics to hymns and songs become dry on our tongues. What once seemed to express our joy with incandescence, now glows feebly. We move on to new songs, only for the pattern to repeat itself. Nothing seems to last.

The problem is not the song, the problem is OUR song.

Using the verses from the great hymn 'A Mighty Fortress is our God', written from Martin Luther's meditations on psalm 46, T. M. Moore helps us recapture our song, written by God's hand in our life.

At trying times Luther would turn to his closest friend and say 'Come Philip*, let us sing the 46th.' May your life also be turned into a more joyful song by staying in harmony with the God of all Creation.

* Philip Melancthon

T. M. Moore is a Fellow of the Wilberforce Forum and Pastor of Teaching Ministries at Cedar Springs Presbyterian Church in Knoxville, Tennessee.

ISBN 1-85792-868-7

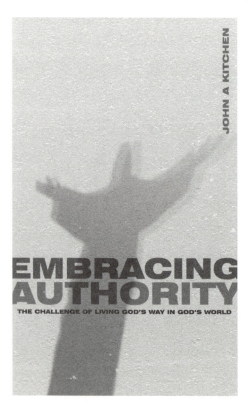

JOHN A KITCHEN

EMBRACING AUTHORITY

THE CHALLENGE OF LIVING GOD'S WAY IN GOD'S WORLD

Embracing Authority

*The Challenge of Living God's Way
in God's World*

John A. Kitchen

'...a thoroughly counter-cultural, transformingly revolutionary, and deeply Christian re-appraisal of the good and wise gift of God-ordained authority structures. Kitchen calls us back to submit to God's mandate of submission and authority in all, but in only, the ways God has designed for his glory and for our highest well being and joy.'

**Bruce A. Ware, President,
Council on Biblical Manhood and Womanhood**

'I heartily commend Dr John Kitchen's thoughtful and unique treatise. I do not know of any book just like this ...eminently Scriptural, relentlessly practical and very well written. I wholeheartedly recommend it.

**David L. Larsen,
Trinity Evangelical Divinity School**

'As a resident of a planet thoroughly saturated with self-centredness run amok, I can think of few topics needing to be discussed more than that of authority.'

**Donald L. Hamilton,
Columbia Biblical Seminary**

'...a perceptive and accurate analysis of contemporary culture together with a robust challenge to the church.'

**Rev. William Taylor, Rector,
St Helen's Bishopgate, London**

ISBN 1-85792-715-X

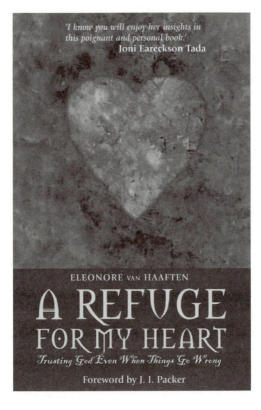

'I know you will enjoy her insights in
this poignant and personal book.'
Joni Eareckson Tada

ELEONORE van HAAFTEN

A REFUGE
FOR MY HEART
Trusting God Even When Things Go Wrong

Foreword by J. I. Packer

A Refuge For My Heart

*Trusting God Even
When Things Go Wrong*

Eleonore van Haaften

'*I know you will enjoy her insights in this poignant and personal book.*'

Joni Eareckson Tada

A Refuge for my Heart takes us into the lives of Naomi, Ruth, Joseph, Leah and David, to discover how they dealt with circumstances outside their power and understanding. We see how the situations they had to face – loss, childlessness, rejection, loneliness – are still common today, and shows us what God's protection really means.

'*All our hearts need constant overhaul, and I cannot imagine the Christian who will not be enriched by what is written here. I commend this book with real and grateful enthusiasm.*'

J.I. Packer

'*This book... has indeed been balm for my soul.*'

Elisabeth Elliot

'*Full of Biblical illustration this is a great resource for leaders and followers alike.*'

Jill Briscoe

Eleonore van Haaften is a producer for Christian radio and TV in the Netherlands, and is a much-respected international speaker.

ISBN 1-85792-684-6

Christian Focus Publications
publishes books for all ages
Our mission statement –

STAYING FAITHFUL

In dependence upon God we seek to help make His infallible word, the Bible, relevant. Our aim is to ensure that the Lord Jesus Christ is presented as the only hope to obtain forgiveness of sins, live a useful life and look forward to heaven with Him.

REACHING OUT

Christ's last command requires us to reach out to our world with His gospel. We seek to help fulfill that by publishing books that point people towards Jesus and help them develop a Christ-like maturity. We aim to equip all levels of readers for life, work, ministry and mission.

Books in our adult range are published in three imprints.

Christian Focus contains popular works including biographies, commentaries, basic doctrine, and Christian living. Our children's books are also published in this imprint.

Mentor focuses on books written at a level suitable for Bible College and seminary students, pastors, and other serious readers. The imprint includes commentaries, doctrinal studies, examination of current issues, and church history.

Christian Heritage contains classic writings from the past.

Christian Focus Publications, Ltd
Geanies House, Fearn,
Ross-shire, IV20 1TW, Scotland, United Kingdom
info@christianfocus.com

For details of our titles visit us on our website
www.christianfocus.com